MACCLESFIELD AS IT W[AS]

by
Robert Home, M.A.(Cantab), Ph.D., Dip.T[P]

"The town is noted for its extensive manufacture of every description of silk goods, including the narrowest ribbon and the best silks, satins, silk handkerchiefs, and plain and figured Gros-de-Naples".

Description of Macclesfield, 1860.

Published by Hendon Publishing Co., Ltd., Hendon Mill, Nelson, Lancs.
Text © Robert Home, 1978.
Printed by Turner & Earnshaw Ltd., Westway House, Sycamore Avenue, Burnley, Lancs.

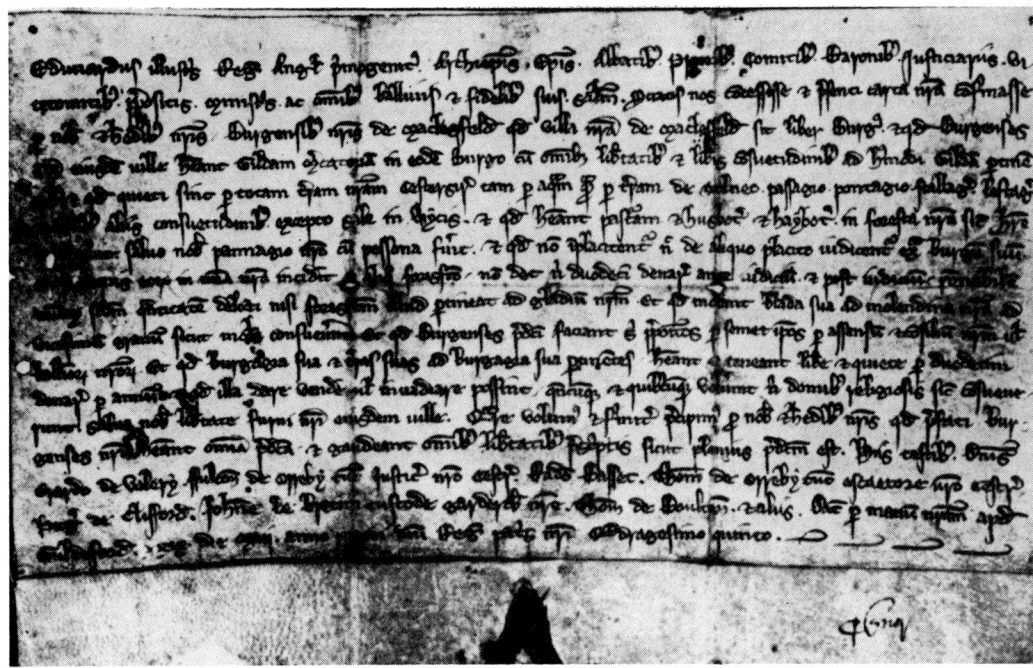

1. Top left. Macclesfield's royal charter: Macclesfield is an old settlement mentioned in the Domesday Book, and in the Middle Ages was the administrative centre for the Hundred, Manor and Royal Forest of Macclesfield. In 1261 King Edward I granted a charter to the town, which made it a Borough, largely free from manorial and other feudal controls, and gave powers of local self-government to the burgesses of the town. The mediaeval town was on the hill above the wooded gorge of the Bollin River, and contained some hundred and twenty burgesses (or men of substance). The origins of the textile industry existed even then. Water power from the Bollin and the Dams Brook was used for fulling woollen cloth (pounding it with large wooden hammers to shrink and felt it).

2. Bottom left. The parish church of St. Michael (originally All Hallows): The building of a church for the town soon followed the granting of the charter: in 1278 Queen Eleanor (whose husband Edward I had given her the manor of Macclesfield some years before) founded the Church of All Hallows, a new foundation subject to the mother church of Prestbury. The church was much altered and rebuilt over the centuries, and considerably damaged in the English civil war. In 1740, with the growth of trade and industry in Macclesfield, it was enlarged and the wooden spire replaced by a stone tower. In 1898-1901 the church was again altered, the present nave built and Gothic ornamentation added to the tower; the design was by Sir Arthur Blomfield, architect to the Bank of England and Eton College. Four kinds of stone were used: Alderley stone for the windows, arches and mouldings, Tegg's Nose stone for the walls, Windyway stone for the steps and paving, and Bollington stone for the tower. The photograph immediately predates the restoration, and shows the Market Place surfaced with a fine expanse of stone setts.

3. Right: The Castle (about 1920): One of the oldest buildings in Macclesfield used to be the Castle on Mill Street. In 1398 John of Macclesfield, an influential courtier of King Richard II and a wealthy burgher of the town, was given a licence "to embattle and kernellate with lime and stone the buildings recently begun in his house or mansion in our town of Macclesfield". Much of the timber used was oak from Lyme Park, and the mansion comprised two courts with a hall, great chamber, parlours and outbuildings. The passage next down Mill Street is still called Palace Yard. Subsequently the mansion passed to the Dukes of Buckingham and then to the Earls of Derby, but it was already in disrepair about 1585, and in 1706 was divided into three tenements. Three shops occupied the Mill Street frontage for over two centuries until in 1933 two of them were redeveloped for a new Marks & Spencer store (now occupied by Mothercare). The third, in spite of the sham front, retains some of the old timbering with wattle-and-daub infilling, and is protected as a building of special architectural or historic interest. The photograph shows part of the ruins of the old castle, demolished to make way for Marks & Spencer; nothing now remains above ground of the old building.

4. Top left: The Sun Inn: At the Market Place end of Chestergate once stood the Sun Inn, formerly the Bull's Head, a fine example of Tudor timber frame construction, dating from 1543. The only fishmarket in the town used to be held in front of the inn. It was demolished in 1864 to make way for a bank building, now in its turn replaced by the National Westminster Bank.

5. Bottom left: The Market Place (about 1900): For centuries before the coming of the silk industry, Macclesfield was a market town serving the surrounding country. Finney, a Macclesfield local historian, described in rosy terms the country people coming on horseback to the market place on market day: "the old farmer seated in front and his better half frequently seated on a side saddle behind him, her basket filled with butter, eggs, etc., to dispose of in one compartment under the old hall, while Darby went to the corn market to transact his business with others in the purchase and sale of their produce; and then, business over, perhaps they would adjourn together to refresh themselves with the good old English fare, of roast beef or an ample supply of brown bread, or oatcake and Cheshire cheese, which they would bring with them, washing down the same with a glass of the 'Best ale under the Sun' as the old swinging sign expressed it, over the old timberbuilt hostelry, called the 'Sun Inn' ".

An ancient Guildhall was demolished in 1823, and the present Town Hall, designed by Francis Goodwin, was built in its place in the Greek revival style. The buildings to the left of the Town Hall, now demolished, included three public houses, the Punch Bowl, the Roebuck and the Old Wheat Sheaf, and the Shambles, where the meat was sold. Opposite, on the corner of Chestergate, stood the bank recently demolished for the new National Westminster building, and the premises formerly occupied by Boots. The Market Place is now a conservation area.

6. Top right: Broken Cross (about 1900): A small settlement existed in Broken Cross from the Middle Ages, earning a living mainly by making baskets and brooms, and it grew after the Common lands began to be enclosed in the 17th century. It was located on the main Chester Road, which improved into a turnpike after 1769. In the 18th and 19th centuries the place became notorious for the Broken Cross gang, who travelled the neighbourhood selling buttons and household items, and also engaged in burglary, pickpocketing and cheating the unwary at local fairs. Similiar activities went on in the neighbourhood of Flash in the hills near Longnor, described by Samuel Smiles in his "Lives of the Engineers" (1862):

"They squatted on the waste lands and commons in the district, and were notorious for their half-barbarous manners, and brutal pastimes. Travelling about from fair to fair, and using a cant or slang dialect, they became generally known as 'Flash men'."

The long-established industry of button-making was even perverted to counterfeiting, for the machines for moulding and stamping buttons could be easily adapted to moulding and stamping false coins.

The famous Brocklehurst family were once associated with the dubious button trade, for their family fortune was started in the 17th and early 18th centuries, when they made buttons at their farm, Gap House, Kettleshulme, and peddled them round the farms of the district. They then diversified into money-lending, and many farmers found themselves mortgaged to the Brocklehursts, as the deeds of farms in the Rainow and Kettleshulme parishes show. These activities provided the wealth for John Brocklehurst (1718-91) to buy into the Macclesfield silk firm of Acton and Street in about 1745, from which the family firm grew.

7. Bottom right: Charles Roe's Silk mill on Parsonage Green (now demolished): Macclesfield moved from the button trade to industrialised manufacturing processes in the mid 18th century. The first industrialised factory unit is generally held to be the silk reeling mill at Derby started between 1718 and 1721 by the Lombe brothers, who had stolen the secret of silk manufacture from Italy in a remarkable piece of industrial espionage. When the Lombe patent expired, other entrepreneurs in the Midlands used their processes, and in about 1756 Charles Roe (1715-74) from Castleton, who had built a mill on Parsonage Green for throwing silk (twisting the fibres into thread), began to apply the new processes. About the same time another mill on the Lombe model had been started at Congleton by a London merchant, Nathaniel Pattison. Roe soon made a fortune from his silk mill, and other large mills were built, like Frost's mill (1785) on the other side of Park Green, and the Card Factory (1785) on Chester Road.

8 & 9. Top left: Charles Roe's windmill, moved to Kerridge (taken about 1920). Bottom left: Alderley Edge copper mine (about 1905): Charles Roe, like many other entrepreneurs of the Industrial Revolution, had a number of business interests, such were the excitement and opportunities of the time. At the same time as his silk mill started, he began copper extraction from the mines at Alderley Edge, and after 1770 extended his mining activities to Anglesey. Roe had acquired land on the former common to the east of the Bollin, and brought the ore to Macclesfield, where a windmill provided the power for crushing it; the ore was then sent to Liverpool for refining. Windmill Street, Windmill Square, Calamine Street, Brasshouse Street, the Smelthouses and Copper Street all preserve the association of that part of the town with Roe's venture, although recent redevelopment has removed some of the names. The venture did not long outlive Charles Roe, as the copper deposits became uneconomic to work, and many years later the windmill was dismantled and reerected on Kerridge Ridge, where it became a prominent local feature. Its eventual sad fate was to be demolished and used as hardcore for air force runways in the Second World War.

10 & 11. Top and bottom right: Inside a silk mill: The 18th century mills were small compared to those that followed, and shortage of working capital limited their productive capacity. The Royal Depot mill, for instance, seems to have been occupied by a number of small enterprises, each with a few employees. The 19th century saw the further development of the factory system, with the limited liability company and the concentration of the control of production in a few hands.

The most important silk firm in the town was controlled by the Brocklehurst family. When John Brocklehurst moved from Kettleshulme to Macclesfield in the 18th century, he acquired interests in the firm of Acton & Street, water rights (the key to textile manufacturing at this time), land in Hursdsfield, and a handsome property on Jordangate, Pear Tree House (which still stands). His son, John Brocklehurst (1754-1839), owned a bank in the town (in the Old Bank Buildings in King Edward Street, which also still stand), one of the small provincial banks which came into existence during the 18th century and provided financial facilities for the Industrial Revolution. Acton & Street was now under Brocklehurst control, and was expanded by John's two sons, John and Thomas, into J. & T. Brocklehurst, one of the biggest silk firms in the country and a rival with Courtauld's of Braintree. The two of them lived in large houses near the firm's Hurdsfield mill, John at Hurdsfield House (now a health centre, its grounds taken for Council housing), and Thomas at Fence House, and another brother, William, had the estate at Swythamley. Although their workers received only a few shillings each in wages, when they both died in 1870 John left £800,000 and Thomas £600,000; this puts their charitable donations into some perspective. When Macclesfield was given two Parliamentary seats by the 1832 Reform Act, John Brocklehurst had one of them until in 1868 he was unseated for corrupt practices.

The photographs show a typical Macclesfield mill in the late 19th century, with predominantly female workers. The attempt to prevent children from working and to regulate working hours and conditions by the Factory Acts was met with extreme hostility by most Macclesfield employers: long hours and the employment of children were both abuses that persisted into the 20th century.

12 & 13. Top and bottom left: Inside Kershaw's mill (about 1910): In the silk trade Macclesfield was prominent in fancy goods such as trimmings, kerchiefs, cravats, and ribbon, and one leading firm in the fancy silk trade was James Kershaw's on Park Lane. Kershaw (1838-1908) was born in Failsworth, Manchester, the son of a handloom silk weaver who operated the first Jacquard loom in the North. His father wanted him to become a teacher, but James became a cutter of pattern cards for the Jacquard looms, and then a pattern designer. In 1864 he moved to Macclesfield, where there were better opportunities in the silk trade than at Failsworth, and took a job at £3 a week (twice his previous pay) as designer at Pickford Street Mills. The firm, Baker, Tucker & Co., were one of the biggest silk manufacturers in the town, and in 1871 employed 1,200 workers, but they later folded completely in one of the periodic recessions in the silk trade. Kershaw started up in business on his own account in 1879, in partnership with George Swindells, a silk throwster from the Royal Depot Mills on Park Green. His enterprise prospered, and was formed into a limited liability company operating from the Paradise Mills, Park Lane, as James Kershaw (Macclesfield) Ltd. He became a leading man of the town, Mayor in 1889, J.P., and President of the Chamber of Commerce, and lived at Summer Hill, on the Chester Road. "The name of Kershaw was one to be conjured with in the fancy silk trade and every buyer knew that if he would anywhere be able to find something new and likely to attract the market, it would be amongst the products with which that name was associated" (Macclesfield Courier and Herald, 4th April, 1908)

The pictures probably show the interior of the Paradise Mill. The mill had whitewashed brick walls with large windows to admit as much natural light as possible.

14. Top right: Packing shirts at Clapham's (about 1910): Some of the Macclesfield textile firms were started by businessmen from Manchester and Lancashire. A cotton spinning mill on the waters was started by "some Lancashire gentlemen" in 1785:

"The business, it seems, was carried on for some time with closed or locked doors, and the workmen were sworn to secrecy. No person unconnected with the works was admitted; only women were permitted to gratify their curiosity with a view of the cotton spinning process; and as the cotton manufacture gave higher wages than the silk throwster could afford, the consequence was a large number of people left the silk for the cotton. To counteract this the silk throwsters had to advance their wages, and in a short time the millmen employed in the silk mills were paid about sixteen shillings a week, on an average the doublers from eight and sixpence to ten shillings, and children 2s.6d., 3s., 4s., and 5s. per week, according to their dexterity." (Finney, "Glimpses of Macclesfield in ye olden days", 1883, p.30).

Cotton never replaced silk as the dominant textile in Macclesfield, but outside firms continued to operate from the town. One such was the Manchester firm of Thomas Clapham (Manchester) Ltd., shirt and blouse manufacturer, which in about 1910 shared mill premises at No. 111 King Edward Street with a firm of silk manufacturers, Neckwear Ltd. The photograph shows shirts being boxed for despatch.

15. Bottom right: Eccleston's, mill engineer, on Park Green: Among the most important workmen in old Macclesfield were the mill-wrights who built, maintained and repaired mill machinery. Samuel Smiles wrote of them in his "Lives of the Engineers" (1862):

"The nature of their business tended to render them self-reliant, and they prided themselves on the importance of their calling. On occasions of difficulty the millwright was invariably resorted to for help; and as the demand for mechanical skill arose, in the course of the progress of mechanical and agricultural machinery, the men trained in millwrights' shops, such as Brindley, Meikle, Rennie and Fairbairn, were borne up by the force of their practical skill and constructive genius into the highest rank of skilled and scientific engineering."

The most famous engineer to be connected with Macclesfield was James Brindley (1716-72), who built the Duke of Bridgewater's canal from Manchester to the Mersey. Born near Buxton, the young Brindley was apprenticed to a wheelwright and millwright at Gurnet, Sutton. Brindley's abilities were first noticed when he worked on the repair of a fire-damaged mill at Macclesfield, and after setting up business on his own at Leek in 1742 he constructed much mill machinery, including the Pattison silk mill at Congleton in 1755, and then moved on to canal work.

The photograph shows the Park Green premises of Edwin Eccleston, "engineer, mill furnisher and general mechanical agent", who appears in the commercial directories between 1874 and 1910. His first premises were at 76 Sunderland Street, and he moved to 40 Park Green.

16 & 17. Top and bottom left: Iron and brass founding at Macclesfield:
The Regent foundry, on Catherine Street, which still stands and is a listed building, produced a number of the beam engines on the Boulton and Watt, model which powered Macclesfield's mills in the 19th century. The 1825 directory shows it occupied by Stringer and Green, brass and iron founders, and for over fifty years it was occupied by the firm of Martin Watts, brass and iron founder, millwright and engineer, among whose many products are the manhole covers and gulley traps which can still be seen in Macclesfield's streets. The upper photograph was taken inside the foundry about 1910. Left to right are Doughty, J.F. Collier (mechanic) and Matthew Collier (engineering foreman). The lower photograph taken about the same time, shows the foundry staff. They include, in the back row, J.F. Collier (3rd from left), E. Clowes (moulder, 5th from left), and seated Robert Sergeant (blacksmith, 2nd from left) and T. Stubbs (foundry foreman, 4th from left).

18. Right: Courtown Foundry, King Edward Street, before demolition:
The other important foundry in Macclesfield was demolished to make way for the speculative office block, Stuart House, and seems to have been started by the Earl of Courtown, hence its name. From about 1860 it was occupied by the firm of Benjamin Harlow and Sons, and they made the cast ironwork for the Arighi Bianchi shop front. After the First World War J.F. Collier, who had served his time at the Watts foundry, took over Harlow's, and his firm still exists, now on the other side of King Edward Street.

19 & 20. Top and bottom left: Stone quarrying near Macclesfield: The stone from the hills near Macclesfield makes an excellent building material, suitable for roofs, masonry or flags, and a visitor to Macclesfield in the 18th century remarked how fortunate the town was to have stone paved streets. Alfred Gatley (1816-63), the famous sculptor, was born at Kerridge, where his father had two quarries, and learned much of his stonemason's skill in those quarries. The largest quarrying firm, Wetton & Sons Ltd., was started by Joseph Wetton at Rainow in the 1850s, and at its most active worked quarries at Windyway, Walkerbarn, Kerridge and Billinge, as well as a steam planing, moulding and saw mills in Grimshaw Lane, Bollington, opposite the Bollington railway station. The work was hard and poorly paid, and profit margins could sometimes be tight: several local firms were bankrupted during the 19th century. The quarry masters frequently worked alongside their men and shared their risks: one master was killed in a fall at his quarry at Water Street, Bollington. Bollington was a centre of quarrying activity, and when Wetton died in 1907 two hundred quarrymen walked in mourning behind the funeral cortege.

The upper photograph shows the Grimshaw Lane Mill, and the lower one the staff at the Walkerbarn quarry. The indentation in the quarry face above the men on the left is the mark left by a "brunt" or iron concretion, which, when weathered down into a sandy substance, apparently was excellent for tomato-growing.

21. Right: The Macclesfield Canal bursting its banks: The Industrial Revolution was accompanied by a revolution in transport — the canals. Charles Roe was active in promoting a canal linking Macclesfield with the River Weaver, but his attempt in 1766 to introduce an enabling Bill at Parliament was blocked by the Duke of Bridgwater, who wanted to protect his monopoly. It was sixty years before a canal through Macclesfield was built, connecting with the Peak Forest Canal at Marple and the Trent and Mersey Canal at Talke, Staffordshire. The line of the canal was surveyed by the great engineer, Thomas Telford, and it was built by William Crossley between 1826 and 1831. Coal could now be brought cheaply to Macclesfield and Bollington from the mines of Poynton, and a number of mills were built along the banks of the canal, notably the huge Clarence and Adelphi mills at Bollington (totalling some half million square feet of floorspace). But the canal made little difference to the prosperity of Macclesfield, for only 14 years after it was opened the railway arrived, and the canal, faced with such competition, was not a successful business venture. This photograph shows the canal, empty of water, when it burst its banks near the Beehive Mill, Bollington, in 1911. The Adelphi Mill is in the background.

22 & 23. Top and bottom left: The railway at Waters Green (also the front cover subject): The canals were superseded by the railways as the new mode of transport, and the railway came to Macclesfield quicker than the canal had done. Only twenty years after the first railway, the Stockton-Darlington line, was opened, and while the railway building mania was at its peak, the first passenger train travelled from Macclesfield to Manchester in November 1845. Macclesfield was unusual in having three railway companies operating out of it: London and North Western, the North Staffordshire, and the Macclesfield, Bollington and Marple. There were also at different times three stations in the town: a temporary wooden station on Beech Lane, the Hibel Road station, and the Central Station (the present station).

The construction of the North Staffordshire changed Macclesfield radically, for (in spite of an unbuilt alternative route which would have passed along the line of Crompton Road) it was carved through the densely populated mills and houses along the Bollin River. The main watering place of the town, on Waters Green, disappeared under a mass of viaducts, masonry and earth works, and a tunnel was driven under Beech Lane. Many buildings were demolished, among which were the original Arighi Bianchi premises.

24 & 25. Top and bottom right: Waters Green Fair: The Waters took its name as the meeting place of the Bollin and the Dams Brook, and was frequently flooded until culverting and other improvements were made. After the coming of the railway a number of hotels were built around the Green for commercial travellers and others coming to the town for business (although few of them still operate as hotels). The two main fairs of the town, Barnaby and the May Fair, were held at Waters Green, and many hundreds of animals were sold at the fairs, especially when the railway made it possible for Irish and Welsh ponies and cattle to be brought long distances to market. In 1902 entries of sheep and cattle at the Wakes Fair totalled 1,699. The top photograph (also the front cover subject) shows the May Fair in 1899: the lower one was taken about 1910.

26. Below. Waters Green from a map of 1874: The closeknit physical structure of the town, with mills, houses, inns, dyeworks, even graveyards all mixed together, is shown in this map of 1874. Inns and commercial hotels are grouped around Waters Green, near both the railway and the cattle market. The graveyard was the principal burying place when the churchyard of St. Michael's became over-crowded; after the cemetery off Prestbury Road was opened in 1866, Queen Victoria Street was built over the graveyard, connecting Waters Green with the lower part of Mill Street. Roylance's occupied the timber yard and sawmill on Boden Street in 1874, but had not yet taken over the lower yard, where the bus station now stands. The dyeworks on the Bollin are now occupied by Scragg's, the textile machinery makers.

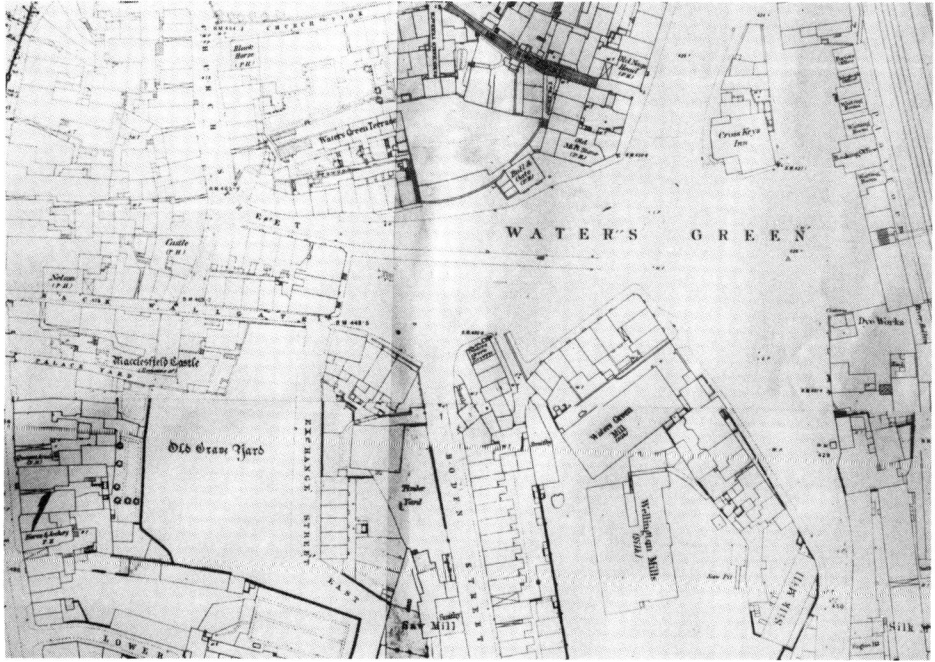

27. Left. George Roylance, Macclesfield's master builder: Many of Macclesfield's important buildings were the work of the firm of George Roylance, which for a hundred years had premises on Waters Green and Boden Street.

George Roylance (1836-92) started as a builder with small jobs around the town, like privies and kitchen extensions, and gradually expanded his activities until he was known as the town's master builder, doing work for the main silk manufacturers, local shopkeepers, the Borough Council, the Macclesfield Equitable and Provident Society, and other clients. His best known contract was the Arighi Bianchi shop front. His firm also provided the hoardings for Macclesfield's celebration of Queen Victoria's Jubilee in 1897, as the account books show:

"1897 June 8 to June 23. Diamond Jubilee decorations Comm^{ee}. To erecting scaffold for West and South Front of Town Hall for Decorations and Illuminations. To use of 216 planks 93 Poles 80 ft boards 298 ropes 36 kerbs 29 padlocks etc. and replacing timber back in yard £45/10/3d."

Roylance died suddenly in 1892 of pleurisy and bronchitis at his home, 63 Brock Street, "highly respected by all classes in the town; from the cottages of the poor, and from our leading men will spontaneously flow a tide of deep and sincere sorrow" (Macclesfield Courier and Herald, 23rd April 1892). His brother Isaac continued the business after his death, and in 1898 a limited liability company was formed to "carry on the business of Joiners, Builders, Timber Dealers, Wheelwrights, Smiths, Plumbers and Dealers in Building Materials, now carried on by the Executors of the late George Roylance". The company was finally liquidated in 1977, and the Waters Green premises (listed as a building of special architectural and historic interest) put forward for redevelopment. The firm's records were saved when the building was cleared, and are now in the safekeeping of the County Record Office, Chester. The site of the firm's lower yard, on the east side of Boden Street, is now occupied by the Crosville bus station.

28. Top right: Macclesfield's men of business at tea. This photograph shows a tea party which took place in about 1872. On the left is a member of the Daintry family (of the Daintry and Ryle bank), third and fourth from the left are the Woodward brothers (active in the silk trade), and on the right Ferdinando Jackson (who with his brother James had the firm of J & F Jackson in Pickford Street and Cross Street). The photograph was taken on a long exposure: unfortunately the dog moved. The garden is believed to be in the grounds of the Conservative Club, Prestbury Road.

29. Bottom right: Workers at Woodward's dyeworks. These were the men who worked for the Woodward brothers at their dyeworks, a few hundred yards from where the tea party was held. The photograph was taken about the same time as the tea party.

30. Top left: Man on a tricycle: This photograph shows a member of the Woodward family on a Rudge tricycle in about 1880. The machine is probably a Coventry Lever or Rudge Rotary tricycle, which was first advertised in 1877. Tricycles were very popular in the 1880s, but fell into decline as safer bicycles came on the market in the 1890s.

31. Bottom Left: The King's School (about 1900): The school was founded in 1502 by the will of Sir John Percyvale, former lord mayor of London, and was originally sited close by the Parish Church. A charter was given to the school by King Edward II in 1552, hence the name, the King's School. In 1748 the school moved to premises in King Edward Street, the site of which is marked by an inscribed stone. In 1856 it moved to the buildings shown in the photograph, purpose built and designed by the architect F. Bellhouse. The area to the front of the buildings is now the King's School cricket pitch. To the right of the photograph is the School Gymnasium (1890), built by George Roylance, in the words of the then Head Master "without any architect, from the dimensions and a rough plan of my own." The original block and the lodge of the King's School are both listed as buildings of special architectural and historic interest.

32. Left: The Sunday School on Roe Street (about 1900): Macclesfield grew rapidly with the expansion of the silk industry: from 5,000 in 1750, to 9,000 in 1800 and 39,000 in 1850. The population in those days was predominantly young, and there were many children in need of school education. In 1796 John Whitaker, the son of a prominent local merchant, started a Sunday school: in only four years it had over a thousand pupils, and by 1812 over two thousand. There was still no proper school building, and it was therefore resolved that "a building capable of accommodating all the children now under instruction, and providing for a moderate increase, be erected in some central part of the town." Following public subscription the Roe Street School was built at a cost of £5,640, the laying of the foundation stone being marked by a public holiday and communal hymn-singing. The building is one of the most striking in Macclesfield, and still stands in spite of major clearance and redevelopment in the area. It is protected as a building of special architectural and historic interest; in the forecourt is a memorial to John Whitaker, who died in 1820.

33. Top right: St. George's School (about 1890): John Whitaker had to fight against strong opposition to keep his Sunday School non-denominational, and after his death sectional jealousies were such that by the 1830s virtually every place of worship had its own Sunday School. A spate of elementary day school building followed, and prominent among these was the St. George's National School, Bridge Street, opened in 1836.

34. Bottom right: Lord Street School (about 1900): Another Sunday School was opened in a vestry of Parsonage Street Chapel in 1820 by a silk throwster, David Oldham, and proved a great success. In 1822 it moved to a new building in Lord Street, which was used for the school on Sundays, and the rest of the week was a silk-twisting room. The Lord Street school, run by the New Connection congregation, was one of the most successful Sunday Schools, which until the 1870 Education Act remained the accepted agencies in the town for educating the children of the poor. In 1869 the cornerstone for a new building was laid by James Jackson, who had been superintendant of the school for 48 years, but in 1911, with the formation of new Council schools, under the 1902 Education Act, the school was closed.

35 & 36. Top and bottom left: Chestergate (about 1900): An important shopping street in the town was Chestergate, so called because it was on the main road to Chester. Some of its buildings are very old, having been altered over the centuries by the addition of new fronts, leaving the older timber frame cores intact. One of these is the Bate Hall Hotel, which was originally a black-and-white courtyard house belonging to the Stopford family of Saltersford. A member of the family, Captain James Stopford (d. 1685) acquired estates in Ireland during the Cromwellian occupation, and his grandson was raised to the peerage as Earl of Courtown, a connection which gave the Courtown foundry its name. In recent years Chestergate has suffered badly from traffic, but the completion of the Churchill Way extension will, it is hoped, make it traffic-free and restore its importance as a shopping street.

37. Top right: Mill Street in 1906: Mill Street has for centuries been one of the principal streets in Macclesfield, although it only acquired its present name in the 18th century, after Charles Roe's silk mill on Parsonage Green. In late mediaeval times its southern limit was set, not by Park Green, but by the town walls (the street name Newgate preserving the memory of the walls) and by the Dams Brook, which is now culverted in that part of the town. Although the main A523 trunk road now runs the length of Mill Street, for centuries the principal north-south road seems to have bypassed the town via Hibel Road (once Cockshute Lane) and Sunderland Street. In the 19th century Mill Street had a bewildering variety of shops, most of them with bow-windowed shop fronts: the shop fronts have changed, but some of the old buildings still survive.

38. Bottom right: Park Green (about 1890): On Park Green lived many of the wealthy men of the town in the early 19th century, and some of the mills were built there. The photograph shows the water fountain presented to the town by James Kershaw, but now demolished.

39. Left. A Macclesfield small shop: Napoleon said that England was a nation of shopkeepers, and certainly old Macclesfield was full of them. In 1850, when the town's population was 39,000, it had more than eight hundred shops. H.G. Wells wrote a jaundiced picture of the life of the small shopkeeper in "The History of Mr. Polly" (1910): "It was soon manifest the shop paid only in the most exacting sense . . . Shops bankrupted all about him, and fresh people came, and new acquaintances sprang up, but sooner or later a discord was inevitable — the tension under which these badly-fed, poorly-housed, bored and bothered neighbours lived made it inevitable." The photograph shows a typical small shop which was probably no more than the front parlour of a two-up, two-down terrace house. The shopkeeper's name appears in the Macclesfield commercial directories between 1906 and 1914.

The pattern of brickwork is common to many Macclesfield buildings of the 19th century, and is made by the different colours of the long and short sides of the brick (the stretchers and headers respectively), a result of the firing process in the brick kiln. The bricks are laid in a Flemish bond, a bond rarely used in modern brickwork because cavity wall construction does not suit it.

40. Left: Charles Hadfield: One of the oldest shops in Macclesfield is Hadfield's, the chemist and drysalter on Churchill Way, which was established in Macclesfield by 1755. The founder was the son of the rector of Hathersage. The first Hadfield shop, in the Market Place, was pulled down in the 1820s as part of the improvements to the Town Hall, and the family then took premises in Dog Lane, where they were for over a hundred years until compulsorily purchased to make way for the Grosvenor Shopping Centre. They moved to their third and present shop in 1966. The photograph shows Charles Hadfield, who managed the shop in the years after the First World War.

41. Top left: West Park, off Prestbury Road (about 1900): After the rapid growth of industrial towns in the first half of the 19th century, the industrialists realised the need for public open spaces for the working classes, who lived in crowded courts and terraces with little access to the countryside. In 1848, following a Royal Commission on the State of Large Towns and Populous Districts, the Public Health Act authorised the establishment of Boards of Health, whose responsibilities included public gardens. In Macclesfield, the Town Field, an area of land set aside for growing hay, was purchased and landscaped, and in Wakes Week 1854 was opened, with great celebrations. It was called Peel Park after the Prime Minister and repealer of the Corn Laws, who had died in 1850, but the name West Park was preferred and it is known by that name today.

42. Bottom left: The Barracks, Crompton Road (about 1900): In 1857 the County Quarter Sessions resolved that a barracks should be provided in Macclesfield for the arms, stores and permanent staff of the Second Regiment of the Royal Cheshire Militia; a site was found in Crompton Road, and the buildings completed in 1858-59. The stone buildings form a square, with the married quarters, the commanding officer's quarters, and an armoury. The barracks were used for some sixty years for the purpose intended, and then the quarters became private dwellings and the Armoury a store for general industrial purposes. In 1977, however, the barracks took on a new lease of life when the Armoury was converted to a club and the whole barracks declared a conservation area.

43: Right: Formation of the volunteer fire brigade in 1863 ("Illustrated London News"): Fire was an ever-present threat in the town, with the quantities of timber used in building, especially in the mills. There were many fires in the town, like the one in 1844 at a mill in Brook Street, which was described by John Earles in his "Streets and Houses of Old Macclesfield":

"The fire broke out between 11 and 12 a.m., and originated in a spark from some machinery setting some cotton ablaze. The flames rose to a great height, and immense crowds assembled in Sunderland Street and on the Sandbank to witness the spectacle. The feelings of the spectators were wrought to a high pitch of excitement when a woman was rescued from the top storey of the burning building by means of a ladder which was placed across the brook." It comes as no surprise that the big manufacturers took the initiative in firefighting, and Charles Brocklehurst (d. 1884) from Fence House organised a volunteer fire brigade with a steam engine given by the Brocklehursts. The engine was nicknamed "the Badger": the Brocklehurst family emblem, a badger, appears on public buildings around the town today, like the Sunderland Street almshouses and the Liberal Hall in Queen Victoria Street, as the visible mark of their munificence. The twelve firemen were volunteers paid by the hour. In 1874 a permanent Fire Brigade was formed under the Borough Surveyor. Until recently, when the new fire station on Chester Road was opened, the fire station was in King Edward Street.

44. Top left: Parkside Hospital (about 1900): Macclesfield's health facilities came to be concentrated to the northwest of the town in the 19th century, and a number of handsome buildings in spacious grounds were erected by endowment and public subscription. First was the Workhouse (now West Park Hospital) on Prestbury Road, built in 1843-45 when the old workhouse on Waters Green (on the site of the present Towns Yard) became overcrowded. In 1868-71 a County Lunatic Asylum (now Parkside Hospital) was built off Victoria Road, large enough to accommodate over seven hundred patients. In 1872 the Infirmary and Dispensary in Cumberland Street was opened; it was designed by the local architect, R. Stevens, and Currey, the architect of St. Thomas' Hospital, London, advised on the scheme.

45. Bottom left: Macclesfield turning out for a procession (about 1910): On public occasions most of the town would turn out for the entertainment. The opening of public buildings and places like the Sunday School and Victoria Park was usually marked by a public holiday and ceremonial processions through the town. For instance, when the Infirmary was opened in 1871, a procession of 8,800 schoolchildren, with the Macclesfield brass band at their head, passed from Park Green to the Town Hall, and there a new procession was formed, composed of the Militia band and staff, the volunteer fire brigade, the volunteer band, javelin men, public office-holders and councillors, the infirmary committee, architect and builder, subscribers to the fund, secret society members, the corporation fire brigade and police. They processed to the Infirmary, where 10,000 people were assembled, and there then followed hymn-singing and public addresses. The photograph shows one such procession passing Jordangate. The occasion is unidentified. The George Inn appears without the reproduction timber panelling which it now has.

46. Left: **Bonfire time at Tegg's Nose**: Signal fire chains were used in times of national danger, like the Armada and Napoleon's threatened invasion, but this fire, at Tegg's Nose, marked a happier event – Queen Victoria's diamond jubilee in 1897.

47 & 48: Top and bottom left: Macclesfield's post office: The main post office in Macclesfield in the late 19th century was on Park Green, where the Co-op building now stands, and this photograph shows the Royal Mail coach by the Sunderland Street entrance in 1897. In 1924 the building was demolished to make way for a new Macclesfield Equitable and Provident Society building and a new post office was built in Castle Street. The lower photograph shows the foundation stone being laid by Mayor D.M. Catlow in 1925. That post office has also been superseded by the new building across the road, and the old building still waits for a new user.

49 & 50. Top and Bottom left: The Arighi Bianchi building, Commercial Road (about 1900): One of the oldest businesses in Macclesfield is the furniture shop of Arighi, Bianchi & Co., whose premises in Commercial Road with their fine cast iron shop front can be seen from the main Manchester-Birmingham railway line. About 1850 two Italian immigrants from Lombardy, Anthony Arighi and Anthony Bianchi, were peddling Italian-made barometers and other items of furniture in the farms around Macclesfield. Italian barometer makers, cabinet makers and glass blowers had been established in many English towns from the 18th century, and several of them seem to have had businesses in Macclesfield as early as the 1820s; one such was John Marie Verga, "carver, gilder and tea dealer" of Market Steeet (1828) and Mill Street (1834). Barometers with the Arighi name still appear occasionally in Macclesfield sale rooms. By 1854 Arighi and Bianchi had formed their own partnership, and for some years they operated from premises in the Waters, behind the Cross Keys public house. They were bought out to make way for the railway, and with the compensation money moved to Commercial Road, where they took over an existing building and added a new shop front in 1882-85. The cast iron facade was made in Macclesfield at Harlow's foundry in King Edward Street; the front and the interior fittings, including a fine showroom staircase, were installed by George Roylance, and the contract is recorded in his account books:

"Contract Statement:

To Erecting New Front (prepared for Glass) to Warehouse, Commercial Road, per Contract 1876.	230. 0. 0.
To New Sign Boards	20. 0. 0.
To New Board and first floor to bottom room	50. 0. 0.
To Plastering walls of first & second storeys	6. 0. 0.
To New Stairs to Show Rooms	26. 10. 0.
To New Grate with oven to houseplace	5. 5. 0.
To plastering portion of ceiling on second floor	4. 16. 6.
To replacing portion of floor in corner of room	4. 0. 0.
To Making good ceiling of lower Room	1. 12. 0
To Extra cost of front gates.	4. 10. 0
Copd Feb 22 1884"	352. 13. 6

51 & 52. Left and right: Granelli's ice cream: In the late 19th century improved methods of production and refrigeration introduced a new confection for the people — ice cream. Italian immigrants were among the first to make and sell it, and by 1890 Angelo Granelli, who had come to Macclesfield from Genoa to join his uncle's sweet shop, Fortonato Granelli of 33 Church Street, was selling ice cream in the streets of Macclesfield. Four generations of Granellis later, the business is still thriving, with parlours at Chestergate and Mill Street. Sheffield and Manchester also have Granelli ice cream, but from different families.

The photographs show the early handcart, and the Dodge ice cream van used in 1919, which was the first ice cream van in the North West.

53 & 54. Top and bottom left: Palmerston Street and Grimshaw Lane, Bollington. (about 1910): While Macclesfield was the main provincial centre of silk manufacturing, Bollington, only a few miles away, was a cotton town closely linked with Manchester and Liverpool. Until the late 18th century there was no Bollington town, only a string of hamlets and farms scattered along the main road from Macclesfield to Pott Shrigley. The Industrial Revolution brought a great change, and the water from the surrounding hills provided the power for several large mills in the Ingersley Vale and down the Dean River. Later steam power and the canal led to bigger mills like the Clarence and Adelphi, and the population of Bollington expanded from 1,200 in 1800 to 4,600 in 1851. The photographs show typical 19th century terraced housing built for the mill workers. While in Macclesfield most 19th century workers' housing was brick built, in Bollington good stone suitable for walls, roofs, floors, and street surfaces was readily available from the quarries. A public house was never far away: both the Hollybush and the Dog and Partridge are still in business (the Hollybush with a mock Tudor front added after the photograph was taken). Palmerston Street was built in the 1860s and replaced the old Pott Shrigley Road, Queen Street, which runs to the left of the Hollybush in the photograph. Bollington in 1900 had no traffic problems!

55. Top left: Bollington town (about 1880): This photograph, taken from the high canal aqueduct which crosses the Dean River, shows the position of Bollington enclosed between hills. To the left is the Congregationalist Church (built in 1867), and behind it the Oak Bank print works (destroyed by fire in 1880). Centre background is the parish church, and most of the mills are to the right, where the Dean is channelled into a number of mill pools and mill races.

56. Bottom left: Lowerhouse, Bollington (about 1900): Lowerhouse, on the Dean downstream from Bollington, was the site of one of the social experiments beloved of 19th century industrialists. A water-powered mill had been built there in the 18th century by the Antrobus brothers, and in 1832 was taken over by Samuel Greg (1804-76), whose father built the famous Quarry Bank mill at Styal. Greg had the idea of creating a complete community around the mill, with terraced cottages and allotment gardens for the workers, and a range of facilities, such as Sunday school, gymnasium, library, reading room, and creche; he even introduced an Order of the Silver Cross for young women of good conduct. He called his model village Goldenthal (or Happy Valley), similar attempts were made by Robert Owen at New Lanark, Arkwright at Cromford, Salt at Saltaire and the Cadburys at Bournville. For fifteen years the project was "his all-absorbing object of consideration and pursuit", but in 1847 the workers, not accepting the submissive role Greg envisaged for them, went on strike when he attempted to introduce labour-saving machinery for stretching cloth. Greg, aggrieved that the proper relationship of master and men had been broken, abandoned the experiment and never went to the mill again, and it eventually passed to Slater Harrison & Co. Ltd.

57 & 58. Left and above: The people of Bollington turn out for Wakes Week: In the first decades of the 19th century Bollington was part of the Prestbury parish and had no church or schools of its own. Fearing the spread of dissenting religion among the working population of the town, the Church Commissioners built a church which was consecrated in 1834, and in 1842 Bollington became a parish separate from Prestbury. In 1839 a handsome Sunday School building (now demolished to make way for old persons' accommodation) was completed near the church, and the photograph on this page shows the Sunday School during Wakes Week, 1913.

59. Left: The main street of Prestbury village (about 1900): Prestbury Parish once included in its jurisdiction some thirty-five townships, including Macclesfield and Bollington, and contained some eighty thousand population until it was broken up into a number of parishes. The church, to the left of the photograph, dates from the 13th century, and reflects in its size and quality the importance of the parish. The black and white building to the right, altered and now a bank, was once the vicar's house.

60: Top right: The New Hall at Gawsworth (about 1900): This was begun by Lord Mohun, but was not completed because he was killed in a sword duel at Hyde Park in 1712. His opponent, the Duke of Hamilton, also died. After lying unoccupied for a time, the building was made habitable, and is now a home for old people.

61: Bottom right: The White Shop, Rainow, in 1906: Rainow village was the site of several water-powered mills, and in the 19th century, having close links with Bollington, enjoyed some prosperity from the cotton trade. At the Rainow end of Ingersley Vale stood Hough Hole Mill (called "the White Shop" from its whitewash), built and run by James Mellor (1796-1891) who lived in Hough Hole House nearby. After Mellor retired the mill was an engineering works, and was eventually demolished, its site now forming part of the grounds of Wayside Cottage, Rainow. The cottages to the left of the photograph were built for workers at the mill, and at the time of the photograph were lived in by two old ladies, who had to walk each week to the workhouse in Macclesfield and back to collect their parish relief of two shillings.

62: Top left: The Cat and Fiddle: The Cat and Fiddle inn, near the highest point on the Macclesfield-Buxton road, and allegedly the highest pub in England, was built in 1830 by John Ryle, banker and MP for Macclesfield from 1832 to 1837, to provide food and shelter for travellers on an inhospitable and frequently snow-bound stretch of road. The road to Buxton had been improved, and turnpiked in 1758. As the photograph shows, the road, in spite of its gradients, was as popular with cyclists in 1908 as now; the basic design of the bicycles in the picture is little different from those of today.

63: Bottom left: Drury Lane, Knutsford (about 1900): At Knutsford are the most flamboyant and imaginative buildings in the Macclesfield area, the hobby of Richard Harding Watt (1840-1911). He was a wealthy Manchester glove maker who used his fortune to develop his fascination with buildings, especially those of Italy, where he travelled widely on business. He was also an enthusiast for the Arts and Crafts Movement of William Morris, which sought a return to the supposed traditional values of the English countryside. At Knutsford, even then an affluent Manchester commuter village, Watt constructed many buildings which combined three very different architectural styles: Manchester classicism, Art Nouveau decoration, and the white walls, plain walls, pantiles and over-hanging eaves of Tuscan villages. Most of these survive, in Legh Road, Drury Lane, and King Street, and some are now protected in conservation areas. The photograph shows the Italian hill village style of the Ruskin Rooms and Drury Lane, both built by Watt.

Ruskin Rooms and Tatton Woods, Knutsford.

64: Right: Industry at Langley (about 1900): Langley village shared in the silk industry, having access to good water power from the hills, and it was a Langley family concern, Whiston's, which joined with Brocklehurst's to form Brocklehurst Whiston Amalgamated Ltd. This photograph shows the tape works at Langley.

65. The King's Head, Gurnett (about 1900), from the canal banks: A last photograph shows the countryside before tarmac and the motor car.